CHILD PRISONER OF WAR

by Hildegard Schmidt Lindstrom

as told to
Hazel Proctor

Proctor Publications, LLC

Published in the USA by
Proctor Publications
PO Box 2498
Ann Arbor, MI 48106

LCCN: 98-67010

Publisher's Cataloging-in-Publication
(Prepared by Quality Books, Inc.)

Lindstrom, Hildegard Schmidt.
    Child prisoner of war : Denmard --WWII / Hildegard
Schmidt Lindstrom, -- 1st ed.
    p. cm.
    Preassigned LCCN: 98-67010
    ISBN: 1-882792-60-2

    1. Lindstrom, Hildegard Schmidt. 2. World War,
1939-1945--Personal narratives, German. 3. World War,
1939-1945--Prisoners and prisons, German--Biography. 4.
Children--Germany--Biography. I. Title

D811.5.L56 1998   940.54'82'43 [B]
                           QBI98-1263

Dedicated
to all the children
throughout the world
who are victims of war.

CHILD PRISONER OF WAR

Table of Contents

Prologue *xi*

Fleeing – Winter 1944 *1*
    On the Farm *3*
    Flight *12*
    Race Against Time *16*
    The *Deutschland* *18*
    Flensburg *20*
    Alpenrade *24*
    Aalborg Vestre Alle – Prisoner of War Camp *29*

Werner – My Story *37*

My Uncle Otto, Aunt Kate and Elly *41*

Prisoner of War Children *45*

Denmark – The War Years *51*

Late Fall – 1947 *57*

Epilogue *60*

Prologue

This story is made up of the memories of a severely traumatized child — almost six decades later. Memories that were too painful to recall earlier. Stories and incidents that are too painful to have never been discussed at family gatherings or passed on to following generations.

Most readers will be unfamiliar with the events being related in *Child Prisoner of War* because the story of thousands of men, women and children being made prisoners in concentration camps <u>after the end of WWII</u> is one the general public has not yet heard.

All the memories are not from the author alone. Family and friends, and research have filled in many of the blanks. Some were related by one person sharing a recalled incident and prompting another memory on a different incident. Telephone conversations between relatives in Germany and Michigan have filled many spots in the story. Photographs that were taken prior to those tragic events have been carefully retrieved from their sixty year old concealed tombs, and loaned to the publisher for inclusion in this book. Family members found it was not easy to look at snapshots taken when the world seemed normal and times were happy. But pictures prompted additional recollections.

The publisher is grateful for all of the assistance. To Dr. J.J. Van Gasse for his explanation of frostbite and how a small child would suffer, especially without medications. To the Proctor Publications staff for historical research and the location of pre-WWII maps, which explained the unlikely route of their journey. To Renee Zepeda for researching the historical role played by the Red Cross in Europe during and after WWII and the role of the United Nations functioning in a devastated Europe. Miss Zepeda also researched the roles of the Danish people during their country's occupation from 1939 to 1945.

To the readers of this book —lest we forget!

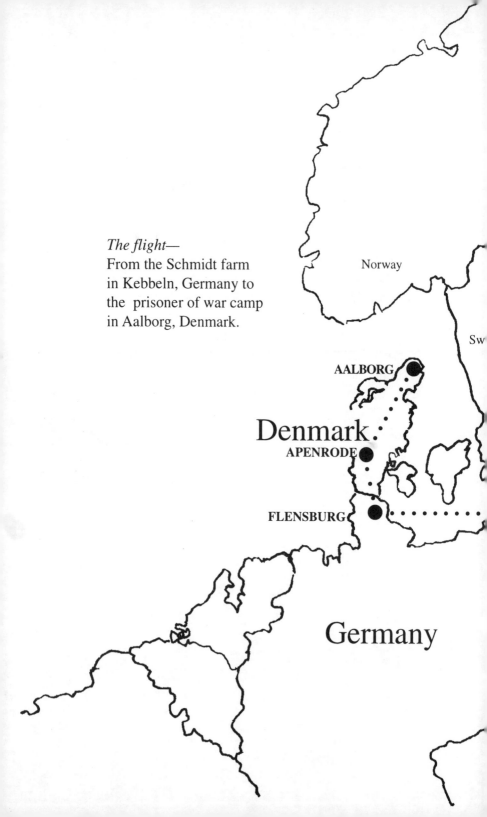

The flight—
From the Schmidt farm in Kebbeln, Germany to the prisoner of war camp in Aalborg, Denmark.

Norway

Sw

AALBORG

Denmark

APENRODE

FLENSBURG

Germany

Fleeing – Winter 1944

I remember mostly the cold. The terrible, hurtful cold. I remember few details of that fateful day, or of the days that immediately followed. But I remember vividly being so cold that I could hardly breathe. Afraid to even move. Afraid that even a small movement would let a tiny bit of the meager heat surrounding my small body to escape and be replaced by additional cold. I was wedged between my mother and father who were trying to protect me from the bitter wind and the –44° weather. But even the warm clothes I was wearing before I was thrown onto the open wagon and the blanket my mother wrapped around me couldn't shield me from the frost-bite that was forming on my face, fingers, and toes — frost-bite that blotched my skin and turned it dark and painful. Frostbite that continued to hurt until I was in my midteens.

I also remember the fear and the hunger — two more realities that still make me shudder almost six decades later. Today, I realize that thousands of small children like myself suffered unmentionable hurts and death in war-torn Germany and throughout Europe. Thousands and thousands of small children who were caught up in a mad world. Mine is but one story. The story of an eight year old German girl living on a farm near the Lithuanian border who fled in terror from the advancing Russian army in 1944.

It is my story and I need to tell it.

On the Farm

I loved to ride Fresco home from school — riding so fast that the wind in my face would force me to squint my eyes as it pulled my pigtails — just like my friend, Ervin, would pull my pigtails to tease me. Sometimes Ervin would ride behind me on Fresco and we'd drop him off at his farm after we passed my grandma's house. He had to get home after school to do his chores, but all I had to do was feed my animals and take care of their needs. Those weren't chores. I loved all my animals and loved taking care of them. Besides my horse, Fresco, I had a black cat named Peter and a dog named Wolf. We had another horse, cows, sheep, and chickens, too, and I got to take care of all of them. I can't remember helping my mother in the house, but then my cousin, Lilly, would help her. She had come to live with us to help on the farm. Lilly was 13, five years older than me.

Some days when my dad needed Fresco to work on the farm, Ervin and I would walk to school. It was a long way. We'd go along the valley where the birch trees grew and through the woods to the clearing where the school house stood in the middle of the playground. It was a country school with only a few rooms for all the grades. I went there for two years because I started when I was six and was only eight when we had to flee. I loved school. My godmother and my aunt were the teachers, so I probably got a lot of extra attention. My father had studied to be a teacher and there were many books in our home. I learned to read early and liked history and geography best. My love of books was probably my salvation during those years I was a child in a prisoner of war camp. We had a small atlas that my father kept hidden under the straw. My father would help me as I read and stud-

ied that atlas. I could tell you the names of all the countries and the forty-eight states in the United States. I even knew the capitals of the states.

My father had purchased our farm in Kebbeln from his father who was no longer able to work the land. Kebbeln is near Memel on the border of Lithuania. We raised wheat and potatoes to sell,

Hildegard and Ervin on their way to school in Kebbeln

besides selling the milk from the cows. Father was badly crippled but he had help with the farm work from some war prisoners the Nazis had put on our farm. These men lived in the barn in a room with hay in it and no beds. I think they were Polish and French. I was supposed to stay away from them, but one of them became my special friend. Neither of them spoke but a few words of German. The French prisoner told me his name was Johnnie and that he had small children at home in France. Sometimes he would receive a small package from his family and then he would share his precious Hershey bar with me. We'd only eat one little square at a time and save the rest for another day. Our family was not supposed to collaborate with these prisoners, but my parents felt sorry for them and often invited them to share our dinner in the kitchen. We had to be very careful because the Nazis would pay surprise visits to the farm to check up on the prisoners. My parents would have been in deep trouble if they found the prisoners in our house.

My horse Fresco had been put on our farm by the Nazis. Johnnie told me he was a French army horse. He only understood French commands. But Fresco and I got along fine. He seemed to know what I wanted before I knew myself. During the weeks before we fled the Russians, Fresco probably saved my life. We were just leaving school one afternoon when a Russian sniper shot at me. Fresco knew just what to do. He took off running fast for home. I didn't even know what had happened until my father told me there were Russian snipers in the countryside and I would not be going to school anymore. I was to stay on the farm.

Our farmhouse was large and comfortable as were most of the farmhouses in that area. It was one story and made of wood and stones from the land. There was a large kitchen with a round table that could accommodate any number of guests. I always liked the good smells of the kitchen. I never had a chance to learn to cook. I guess mother and Lilly didn't need an eight year old in their way while turning out those good stews, breads and pies. Living on the farm, we always had plenty to eat. However, I can remember sneaking up to my grandmother's house and asking her for pieces of her rye bread. I'd tell her I was hungry because we didn't have any food at our house. She'd smile with a twinkle in her eye and give me a slice of warm fresh bread. I still remember how good that bread tasted. I don't know why I told the fib about our not having any food. I think it was just a game I played with my wonderful grandma. My grandmother's warm rye bread was one of the things I fantasized about when I was so hungry in the prisoner of war camp. For days at a time, we'd only have a watery barley broth to eat. I'd pretend that broth was the thick beef and vegetable soup that grandmother would serve in her wonderful smelling kitchen. And, of course, I'd pretend to have a slice of fresh rye bread to dip into it. I never saw my grandmother again after she had to stay behind in Konigsberg. But I'd pretend she was waiting for me somewhere. It is very hard for a child to face horrible reality, even as she is living it.

Birch trees have always held a special attraction for me. From the time I was a very small child, the clump of birch trees in the yard overlooking the valley was my secret dreamland. I was sure the fairies I'd known about since I was very young lived there. I'd spread my blanket under those graceful trees that seemed to be reaching for the sky, and watch the clouds go by as I dreamed the dreams of a small, imaginative girl. I was going to be a teacher, but only after I'd visited all those exciting places my father and I

Lilly, Edertraut and Hildegard on the farm

read about. I'd teach children about the strange clothes Japanese children wore, and the eskimos' houses of ice in Alaska. But, of course, the children would have to learn to read and write first. I would play school there beneath my birch trees. My young cousin, Edertraut, and my dog, Wolf, were my pupils. Edertraut would sit for hours as I "taught" her to read and write, and learn to recite poetry. Wolf usually lost interest after a short time. But Edertraut was only four years old, and my "teaching" entertained her. Edertraut and her mother were living with my second grandmother while her father was away at the war.

There was a stork nest on our farm that I could see

from my birch trees. I would watch the storks and wonder if they would bring me a sibling of my own. I would talk to them in whispers and beg them to bring me a baby brother or sister. But it didn't work. I didn't get a baby sister or brother. I really thought it would work since I was begging them from my magic trees.

There were many birch trees in the valley. I could watch the wind move the branches in the afternoon sunlight. I thought it was my special magic show to watch. My father and I would go there to hunt for mushrooms, and in the spring we'd pick the white, delicate Lilies of the Valley. One afternoon, my mother had gone into the valley alone to see after the cows. Suddenly, a wolf sprang from the woods and attacked her. Fortunately, she was carrying a large stick and struck at him. He quickly ran from her and disappeared into the woods. She was very frightened by the wolf. We'd never seen one in our area before. My father said it was because of the fighting across the border in Lithuania that the wolves were being driven into our country. I didn't understand it. I knew we were having a war, but I was taught in school that we were winning — Mr. Hitler, the Führer, said so — and there was nothing to worry about. I knew my parents were very uneasy and careful whenever the Nazi SS came around, but I didn't know why. I was always sent to my room and told to be quiet. It was a puzzle, but I had more important things to think about than wolves that didn't know who was

Hildegard and Ervin sit on either side of Grandpa Schmidt. Lilly, little Edertraut, Aunt Elly and two unidentified children make up this Sunday gathering.

winning the war.

My grandfather was a special person to all the children in the family as well as the neighborhood children. On Sunday afternoons he would spread a large blanket on the grass and sit in the middle so all of us children could sit close to him. He had a musical instrument that looked like a small accordion. He could play anything on it. He'd sing the old songs he'd learned as a child, or he'd make new, silly ones to teach to us. Sometimes my grandmother and other adults would join in singing the old traditional songs. It was a very special Sunday when my Aunt Kate and Uncle Otto would visit. They were my mother's aunt and uncle, which made them my great aunt and uncle. It didn't matter to me. They were special even if Aunt Kate was grumpy looking and seldom smiled at us children. Aunt Kate had a wonderful voice and would sing songs from operas. My mother said she could have been an opera star if she had wanted to and studied hard enough. She looked a lot like an opera star I saw in a magazine. Aunt Kate was very large. She was tall and she was fat, but mother said that even though she weighed well over 190 pounds, she kept herself corrested, whatever that meant. When I asked what corrested meant, mother told me I was too young to know. Sometimes my father would sing a duet with Aunt Kate. It was so beautiful. Everyone else would be very quiet and just listen. It was the only time I ever heard my father sing except when we all sang together. Even though I am grown now and have lived in the United States for many years, tears come to my eyes whenever I hear any of those old songs. Sitting on that blanket close to my grandfather and singing songs is a grand memory.

My grandfather was a cabinet maker, although since the war began he mostly made caskets. I loved the smell of the wood as he sawed and pounded the boards into a box. My favorite was when he would use his plane and make wooden curls as he smoothed the edge of a board. He'd gather the golden curls and attach them to my braids and tell me I was his princess. Our homes had beautiful furniture my grandfather had made, but there was no time for making grand furniture when the German army needed caskets. When we had to flee the Russians, my grandfather had to stay behind to fight them. The German soldiers said he was "able bodied" and was needed. I never saw him again after we left in the wagon. I guess he was killed by the Russians.

I didn't like having to stay home from school. I missed my friends and my lessons. Most of all I missed riding Fresco as he galloped through the early winter afternoons. I rode him everyday on the farm when he wasn't having to work with my dad, but it wasn't the same.

One day, soon after I could no longer go to school, Lilly and I were walking in the frozen potato fields. The leaves of potato plants are quite large and it was fun to feel the crunch of the frozen foliage under our boots. We were playing a jumping game where we'd jump among the patches and see who could make the loudest crunching sound. We heard some airplanes flying close by. Suddenly, Lilly roughly pulled me to the frozen ground with her and we huddled together as one of the planes dove towards us and strafed the potato field where we were. The sound of bullets hitting the ground only a few yards from us was frightening. The plane flew on and didn't come back so Lilly and I ran for the house. When we got there, father told us to get in the farm wagon, quickly, quickly. I had no idea what was happening, but I recognized fear for the first time in my young life.

Flight

I scarcely remember what was loaded in the wagon with us, but it was only the few things my parents had quickly gathered together — some food, extra clothing and a couple of blankets. My mother and cousin were crying, but since I didn't know what was happening, I felt excited, like we were going on an adventure. No one had time to talk to a little girl, but my mother held me very close as we drove out of the farmyard and I became aware that something bad was happening. We were leaving the farm and all my beloved animals, and my magic birch trees. Our prisoner workers stood in the distance and watched us leave. Johnnie gave us a half wave. We never learned what happened to them. I have always wondered if Johnnie ever got home to his children in France.

When our wagon got to the road, we joined a train of many wagons — other families leaving their homes and farms to flee the advancing Russians. Grandmother was waiting at the side of the road when we got to their home. She quickly climbed on our wagon, but grandpa just came to each of us and kissed and hugged us good-bye. He held me for only a few seconds, whispering, *"Liebling, mein schatz,* (my little love, my treasure), remember that I'll always love you," then dad spoke to the horse and pulled the wagon back into the wagon train. As we were pulling away, I screamed and cried for my grandfather and told him to get on the wagon. But he stood where we left him — just watching us, not even waving. My school friend, Ervin, stood near him. Although he was only a young boy, the German soldiers said he would be needed to defend the "Fatherland", as was my grandfather. I only remember my grandmother holding me tightly and we cried and sobbed together until I could cry no more. We never heard anything definite about the fate of my grandfather or Ervin. As the wagon train moved on, someone in a wagon ahead of us started singing, *"Aufweidersehen Mein Lieb Heimatland"* — (Till We See You Again, My Beloved Homeland). Voices joined in from every wagon. My sobbing had stopped, but a terrible fear gripped my heart.

My father was one of the few men not left behind to fight the Russians, because he had only one arm and badly crippled legs. The wagon train kept moving day and night. Other wagons joined us, but the traveling was slow. We slept and ate in the wagons and seldom left them. I was terribly cold. Even the weak winter sun did little to raise the $-44°$ temperature. At night, we could not protect ourselves from the bitter cold in that open wagon. A few German soldiers were with us, but they were concerned with our slow pace. The Russians were advancing faster than they anticipated.

After a few days, we came to a refugee camp. It was only one large room with straw on the dirt floor. At least we had a roof over our heads for one night. We were given some hot broth and bread by Red Cross workers. It was the first hot food we had had since leaving the farm. I'll never forget how good it tasted. The room was very crowded with all the families from the wagon train, and we had no light or lanterns. Although it was a little warmer, the noise of crying babies and children, moaning people who had left loved ones behind, and others being sick, made even an exhausted sleep very difficult. It was the first night of our family sharing very crowded quarters with strangers. It became a way of life for us for almost three years.

The next morning, we were loaded onto army trucks that our German soldiers had located. We were still very crowded, but the trucks had a canvas top and sides that protected us from the bitter wind. We couldn't see out, so we didn't know where we were going. My father talked with the soldiers and they told him the Russians were very close behind us. We stopped again after a few days and again were given some hot food by Red Cross workers. I was very hungry, but mostly I was cold and afraid. That night, the soldiers herded us quickly into the shelter and told us no one was to leave. They sped off in the direction we had come from. After awhile, we heard two explosions and what sounded like gunfire. Everyone was very frightened. Finally our soldiers came back and told my father that they had been able to waylay two Russian tanks that were on the road. They had planted explosives and were able to explode both tanks. They killed the Russian soldiers who tried to escape. They said we were in great danger and everyone must be ready to leave again at daybreak.

This time we didn't stop until we reached the outskirts of Konigsberg. The Red Cross had a larger camp ready for us and more hot food. We ate sparingly of the food from the suitcase my mom had brought from the farm. She tried to save it for when she knew we would need it later.

It wasn't quite dark and I asked my father if I could go outside for a few minutes. The countryside was pretty, with trees and rolling hills, and the town of Konigsberg looked larger than any I had ever seen. For a short while, I forgot my fears and sorrow and thought of my birch trees. I guess I was daydreaming because I never saw the Russian plane that dove out of the clouds and shot at me. I screamed in terror and rushed back to my father.

That night, the Russian planes bombed Konigsberg. The sky was lit by the bombs and the fires that burned through the night. One of the country's largest paper factories had been hit. The next morning, our camp on the outskirts of the city was covered with bits and pieces of paper, as if it had snowed during the night. The city of Konigsberg was completely destroyed in one night.

Three of our trucks had been hit and couldn't be driven. There wasn't room for all of us to go on. The soldiers made the decision that the old people would have to be left behind — which included my grandmother. I didn't think I could hurt any more, but I did when I kissed and hugged my beloved grandmother for the last time.

Race Against Time

We lived in terror. We could hear the sounds of bombs, cannons, airplanes, and sometimes machine gunfire and rifle shots. It seemed the war was all around us, but daddy said the German soldiers who were trying to get us to safety knew where we were going. I'm not sure how long it took us to reach Gotenhafen, on the Gulf of Danzig. I was numb. Daddy kept encouraging me to stay strong, saying we had each other and if we could stay together, somehow we'd make it through. He'd tell me he needed to see me smile, because it gave him the strength to keep going. I couldn't smile, but I always tried for him anyway. I clung to him now. I needed to touch him all the time.

In Gotenhafen there was a large crowd of people just like us — families, mostly without men, who were trying to get away from the advancing Russians. One of our soldiers told daddy where the gangplank would be for the ship we were going to try to get on, and daddy steered us in that direction. The crowd of people was pushing and shoving in every direction. We were all being crushed and I thought I was going to suffocate. Mother, Lilly, daddy and I held onto each other tightly as we slowly made our way to where the soldier had directed us. A little girl to the side of us stumbled and her mother stooped to pick her up. The crowd of people pushed over them and crushed them to death. They didn't even have time to cry out. Others who were being trampled to death screamed, but there was no one to help them. The sounds of their screams rang in my ears. Those screams stayed in my nightmares for many years. Even today, I will wake up from a nightmare, hearing those screams.

   We finally made it to the wharf and saw the ship we were to sail on. It was a freighter called the *Deutschland*. It had three decks where cargo could be stored. Now it would carry people. We learned that another freighter carrying people had hit a mine the night before and all the people drowned. The *Deutschland* was the last available freighter and this was to be its last trip across the Baltic Sea to northern Germany. The ship was almost full of people when we got to the gangplank. Daddy pushed me ahead of him onto the deck with Lilly coming just behind him. I clung to the rail and saw my mother still on the wharf. She had lost Lilly's hand and got shoved to the side. She wasn't able to reach the gangplank. I was hysterical. I screamed and screamed and attracted the attention of one of the busy sailors. He asked me who was my mother, and I screamed at her to wave to us. He threw her a rope and helped my dad pull her up the side of the ship onto the deck. I didn't think I could stop crying when I grabbed onto her, I was so scared. My dad gave the sailor his last cigarettes. I'll never forget the little smile the sailor gave me nor his slight tug on my hair, as if to say everything was all right now, I could stop crying.

The *Deutschland*

There was no more space on the ship. We were one of the very last families to get aboard. There was tremendous confusion. We couldn't possibly move more than a few feet from the spot where we stood after my mother was hauled aboard. Since many people were still standing, dad was able to push us over to a wall, and told us all to sit down. We at least had something to lean against. Many people didn't have any protection as they huddled together in small groups. The gangplank was hauled up and we eased away from the dock. It was pitiful to see the faces of those being left behind. There was no more yelling or pushing forward now. Even the injured fell silent. And the faces became blank as resignation took over the emotions of the crowd. We recognized faces of families that had traveled with us in the trucks. Daddy and mommy whispered together about the sadness of having to leave so many to face the advancing Russians. We couldn't see the German soldiers that had been so kind to us since we left the farm. My dad had gotten to know several well. One was from a small town not too far from Kebbeln, and he knew my grandfather. These men were like most of the people we knew. They were soldiers fighting for our homeland. We hadn't seen any of the Nazis SS since the sniper shot at me and Fresco and dad got word of the Russian advancement.

Although we were on the ship as it sailed out of the Gulf of Danzig, new horrors awaited us. We had no food and there was none for us on the ship. My mother's precious suitcase that held our clothes and a little food had been lost in the crush of getting on the ship. We had nothing but the clothes on our bodies. We had had little to eat since we dashed from Konigsberg. The Red Cross had handed bread and sometimes apples to the soldiers as they paused for gasoline for the trucks. But there was never enough to go around. We broke the bread in pieces and tried to save some for morning. The soldiers had brought us buckets of water to drink from the nearby streams. Now we were very hungry, as well as afraid and cold. No one knew how long it would take for us to reach safety.

The *Deutschland* sailed into the Baltic Sea, but we felt anything but safe. At night, we sailed without lights for fear of attracting a Russian submarine or ship, and the danger of hitting a mine was always present in our minds. The sailors would look for mines in the choppy waters, but it did little good to keep watch at night.

We had no food or water that first night. In the morning, the sailors distributed a little water. These men were not as kind as the soldiers we had been traveling with. Perhaps they were overwhelmed by the large number of people crowded on every available space of the decks. The ship had no toilet facilities, and we soon found ourselves with another horror. People relieved themselves where they were. The decks were built for cargo, not people. There were wide spaces between the planks, so the human excretions and vomit fell on those of us on the lower deck. We had nothing to cover ourselves with, so my mother placed Lilly's and my heads beneath her skirt. We traveled that way most of the time. We welcomed the occasional wave that would wash over the deck, even though the cold water added to our misery. Cold, fear, and hunger had become our way of life. After awhile, you become numb. Daddy continued to talk to us and encouraged us to be strong — to hold on. Someday, he promised, all this would end.

Flensburg

The *Deutschland* finally reached the safety of Flensburg in the very north of Germany. The war was raging everywhere, but we had escaped the advancing Russians. I had to be carried off the ship. I could not walk, and my mother, dad, and Lilly were too weak to carry me. I remember the strong arms of a German soldier as he gently carried me down the gangplank. He too whispered words of encouragement to me, telling me it was over and I was safe now. I don't remember getting to the center the Red Cross had set up for the crowds of refugees pouring into Flensburg. I remember some hot soup offered by kind hands. Mainly I remember the bath my mother and a nurse lowered me into. The water was cool at first, but after I had soaked awhile, tepid water was added, and finally warm comforting water helped me to thaw. The frostbite was very painful, but the water was soothing and the soap that caressed my body and washed my hair smelled sweet. I forgot the stench of the ship as I lay in the water. There weren't many tubs to accommodate the crowds waiting to use them, so Lilly climbed in with me to take her turn in the warm bath, so I could stay and enjoy the water for a few moments longer. We had no change of clothes, but the Red Cross ladies found some donated things to give us. The boots I was wearing had to be cut from my frostbitten feet. I can still remember how much it hurt. Clean socks and soft slippers were given to me. It took me a few days to learn to walk again with the help of mom or Lilly. I had a dress much too large for me, but it was clean. I was still very weak, but I began to feel better and was soon able to get around by myself. I felt strange in my large slippers that were kept on my feet by wide ribbons or old ties that were tied in bows on the tops of my feet. The Red Cross ladies tried to cheer me up with their colorful decorations for my slippers.

We stayed in the refugee camp in Flensburg for a couple of weeks. Dad, mom, and Lilly had also suffered during our trip, as did everyone on board. They too suffered frostbite but not as seriously as me. We welcomed the time to rest and eat the food being given to us. Slowly, our family regained its strength and limited health, although we'd lost a lot of weight. Most of the refugees had fled from the south by land. The *Deutschland* was the last ship to cross the Baltic Sea with refugees. It was torpedoed one evening when we were close to Flensburg but the freighter was able to limp into port. The soldiers and Red Cross people called it a miracle that we'd made it safely. All ships were being sunk by submarines or bombed.

There was much talk of the war and how it was progressing. Most felt Germany was winning. I was confident we were winning. After all, I was taught in school that the Führer was good for Germany and did everything right for us. I didn't understand why we had to flee from the Russians, and my dad was reluctant to talk to me about it. He didn't salute and say *Heil Hitler* unless a soldier said it to him first. We had been taught that every good German said *Heil Hitler*, but it didn't bother me if my dad didn't want to. There were no Nazis SS in Flensburg. Everyone said they were winning the war in the south.

My dad and I walked around the town and went down to the wharf to see the Baltic Sea. I enjoyed the trees and houses of the town, but I didn't like the water. My memories were too fresh. Sometimes we would hear bombs or cannons in the distance, but it wasn't frighteningly close. Airplanes flew overhead from a nearby airfield, but we saw the swastikas on their wings and knew they belonged to us.

Dad made inquiries and tried to find out what had happened to the people left behind — grandpa, grandma and the rest of the family. Lilly's family lived near Aunt Kate and Uncle Otto in another town further west from Kebbeln. Dad could not get any information. The Red Cross promised to try to reach relatives for the refugees, but we never heard anything for several years until after the war had ended. We never learned what happened to grandpa and Ervin in Kebbeln, but daddy was told to assume they had been killed. The Russians did not take prisoners. Grandma was also killed along with those left behind in Konigsberg. My dad tried to fill my mind with other things, and not think about those we'd lost. He kept saying we don't know for sure — we'd have to pray for their survival. I no longer wanted to be strong for him, but he told me that my grandpa also wanted me to be strong, so I tried and tried.

The time we spent in Flensburg, Germany was a time for healing. The Red Cross ladies gave each of us clothes, shoes (slippers for me) and a warm coat. Nothing fit, but that didn't matter. They also gave mom needles and thread, which proved to be invaluable when we became prisoners of war.

Dad had found a small atlas, and we again were able to play our game of finding places to visit around the world. This little atlas was the one he kept hidden under the straw when we were in the concentration camp in Denmark.

One morning, we were told to go to the train station — we'd be traveling to Alpenrade in Denmark. Germany had occupied Denmark since 1939.

Alpenrade

The train was very crowded and we had to sit on the floor some of the time. But we had been given food to take with us and the trip was uneventful. I enjoyed the trees, fields and little towns as they rushed by, and my dad told me stories about the interesting things I was seeing.

Alpenrade was a nice town. We were free to go and do as we wished. The streets were busy and the stores were very inviting. However, we had no money, so all I could do was look in the shop windows and wish for the things I saw. One store had a lot of dolls in the window. There was a special doll that I thought was beautiful and I wanted it so badly. It had long blond, curly hair and she had a pink dress with shoes to match and little white socks. She had lacy underclothes that I could see under her dress. She had a sweet smile and big blue eyes. I was sure that if I could hold her,

her eyes would close. I hadn't wanted to play with dolls on the farm because I had my animals, but I wanted that doll for my very own. I never got it.

The refugees were put in a nice Danish hotel, but it was crowded. There were only three stories and we were on the second floor. Two families shared one room with two beds. It was difficult for our family of four to share our one bed and the small space on our half of the room. But we managed. We were given bedding and pillows that we could wash and keep clean. It was importent that the socks I wore under my slippers be very clean to prevent infection. My frostbite hurt and I would cry a lot, especially at night. I tried to be quiet when I cried because I didn't want to disturb everyone, but the two small children in the other family also cried a lot, even though they didn't have frostbite. They had nightmares.

My mother found work with a German army family stationed in Alpenrade, which gave us a little money. She bought material and sewed clothes for us by hand. But, there was no money for the doll.

All the refugees ate together in the dining room of the hotel. German soldiers brought us food, which the women cooked. We ate well. I remember good breads and special cookies someone's mother would bake for us. Baths were not a problem and we were able to wash our clothes. As soon as the novelty of being free in a new town wore off, I got bored. Lilly had made a friend and spent most of her time with her.

My dad resumed my studies, which I enjoyed very much. We'd play our atlas game and dad would give me history lessons about the places we'd "visit." He'd make every place in the world sound exciting.

There were a lot of other children among the refugees, several of my age. One boy had found a piece of chalk in his pocket and we made a hopscotch game outside on the walk. We'd play hide and seek in the nooks and crannies and the halls of the hotel. The adults didn't seem to mind our loud noise or laughter. Our noise must have been sweet music to the parents of children who had just come through such horror. It is amazing how resilient children can be. I never played at anything for long because my frostbite would start hurting. I would mostly sit still and watch the others.

I was taken to an army doctor to see what could be done for my frostbite. The skin on my face, fingers and toes had turned dark — almost black in some places. It still hurt a lot. He gave my mother Zinc Oxide and Vaseline to put on it, but it hurt when she applied it. A warm bath felt best. The doctor told my mom and dad that he thought he could save all my toes and fingers, and that my face would eventually heal, but it would take years. Skin would flake off and my fingers or toes would become more sensitive. It took a decade for the frostbite to completely leave me. Even today, six decades later, if I'm in a Michigan winter wind, my face will tingle and become unusually sensitive.

I missed our home and my animals. My dad asked if there were a zoo in the city where he could take me, but was told that it had been closed several years ago. There was no food for the animals. The only animal I saw was a dog named Heidi; she belonged to one of the soldiers who brought our food to the kitchen. I'd watch for his truck and run down to see Heidi. The soldier said she was going to have puppies, and maybe I could have one if we ever moved away from the hotel. I dreamed of that little puppy I might get someday. I even picked out a name for it. I didn't tell anyone — not even my dad — that I might get a puppy of my own. I guess I knew that, like the doll, I couldn't have it.

There was a wide curving staircase that led from the second floor to the lobby of the hotel. Some of the boys would slide down the banister. It looked like a lot of fun, but I was afraid I'd hurt my frostbite. Lilly and her friend would walk down the staircase pretending to be great ladies. They didn't have any fancy play clothes to dress up in, but they didn't need them. They had fun pretending. Lilly, who was like my big sister, didn't want a little sister interfering with their fun. I had to sit and watch, as usual.

My birthday was on April 6th — I turned 9 years old. My mom made me special sweets and we had a party with all the children. Everyone sang and it was a special time. Of course there were no presents, but it didn't matter. I was happy for a little while.

One month later, on May 7th, 1945, the world again became a very ugly place for us. At 2:41 a.m., in a modest school house at Rheims, Germany surrendered to the Allies. May 8th became the historical V-E Day.

I was standing at the top of the staircase that morning when I became aware that everyone was very quiet listening to the radio in the lobby. I knew something bad had happened again. The radio said that the war was over. Germany had lost the war. Our "beloved" Führer was dead. Loud noise burst from the throats of everyone in the lobby. Most were crying and screaming. I cried also. I had been taught in school that the Führer was the greatest man on earth and that he'd win the war. My world collapsed, again. Arguments broke out between the refugees — some were happy the war was over, but others were bitter.

My dad and mom said very little and quietly took me back to our room. They told me that people were shouting and angry because the war had ended. Some were glad it was over even though Germany lost, and others thought it was a disgrace that Germany had surrendered. What it meant to us was that the war was over. The fighting had stopped. Dad said maybe we could go home now — back to our farm. Back to my birch trees.

Aalborg Vestre Alle – Prisoner of War Camp

The chaos continued. The soldiers didn't bring groceries and the women didn't go to the kitchen to cook any meals. Mom went down and brought back some bread and fruit from the day before. We had a meal in our room. Dad told Lilly and me to stay in the room. We watched from the window as crowds of rejoicing Danish people celebrated in the streets. They sang their national anthem — *Der er et Yndgt Land* (A Lovely Land is Ours) — hugged each other and danced. Dad went out to try to find out what provisions would be made to get us back home. He could not find any German soldiers on the street, let alone anyone in authority.

Denmark had been occupied by the Germans for six years, and now their country was free — free from the hated Germans that had occupied their beloved homeland. I felt happy for these people as I watched. We opened the window so we could hear their singing and laughter. I had no way of knowing that the rejoicing of these happy people would portend two and half years of misery and cruelty for us.

Dad returned and whispered something to mom. They quietly discussed what he had found out and I recognized the looks on their faces. That terrible feeling of foreboding returned. I knew that something bad was about to happen. Dad said to quickly gather our few belongings and to put on our sweaters and coats. Within a few minutes, there was angry pounding on the door and it was pushed open by several men. We were herded down the stairs with the other families. We were told to get aboard a truck that was in front of the hotel. Some children were separated from their mothers, and the Danish men roughly threw them into the nearest truck, not trying to get them with their families. People stood on the sidewalks and jeered at us as we got on the trucks. I didn't understand their anger. These were the same people I'd seen on the streets when I walked around the town. I recognized the lady that had the doll store. She had invited me into her store one day so I could see my doll up close, and peek at the lacy underclothes. Today she was screaming bad things at me.

The angry men would not let us take anything with us other than what we were wearing. Our clean sheets, towels and blankets were left behind, as well as the extra dress mom had sewed for me and my few little belongings. If dad had not told us to wear our coats, we'd not have had anything warm to wear. Many families were taken completely by surprise and did not have time to dress warmly.

We were very crowded in the trucks. The Danish men didn't seem to care how many of us they crammed into each truck. Dad said they were German army trucks that they'd probably gotten from the army camp in town. The canvas sides were rolled up and the crowds continued to jeer at us as we rode out of town. We saw other trucks carrying German refugees. We drove all night and well into the next day before we reached the city of Aalborg, in the north of Denmark.

We were roughly herded into an empty army barrack. The day before, it had been a German army barrack on an airfield. We never knew what happened to the soldiers stationed there. Maybe they flew to safety when Germany surrendered, or maybe they were captured by the Danes. One disabled airplane was left on the field. Everything had been stripped from the interior of the barrack and dirty straw had been scattered on the floor for us to sleep on. The bunkbeds, tables, chairs, bedding and other items you'd expect to be left in abandoned barracks had been taken away. We were left with nothing, not even a bar of soap. There was water in a single latrine, so we were able to quench our thirst. We had not eaten since the morning before, and we were all feeling the pains of hunger — the same familiar pains we had felt as we had fled the Russians.

Many truck loads of people were pushed into the barrack we were in until the large empty room was crowded. Dad found us a small corner and we sat down, waiting for we knew not what. Everyone spoke in hushed tones, with mothers quietly asking if anyone had seen a child that was missing. We heard padlocks being put on the doors, and without any lights or comforts of any kind, we tried to settle in for the night. There was no heat and the wooden floors were covered with only a thin layer of dirty straw. Our prisoners on the farm had slept in the barn on clean, sweet smelling hay, and my mom gave them clean bedding and plenty of good food. We had no blankets, and we were cold and hungry. Dad again whispered encouragement to me, calling me his *kleine spatz* (small sparrow), and told me to stay his brave girl. He told me this too would end and we'd go home to the farm. The numb feeling I'd felt on the *Deutschland* returned. We were not safe after all.

The next morning, the doors were unlocked and several Danish soldiers came in. We were each given a cup of foul-tasting barley soup. It did little to assuage the hunger we felt. Then a Danish officer told us the rules we were to follow. The most important being that anyone trying to escape from the encampment would be shot. He said we could leave our building and walk around the yard. He warned that the camp was completely enclosed by high barbed wire, and patrolled by Danish soldiers with orders to shoot to kill. Everyone was to be housed in the barrack they'd been placed in. If children who were separated from their mothers were found in another barrack, they could be moved to the mother's barrack. This was the only concession to decency this man made. He said we'd receive food twice a day. He didn't say that the food would only be watered barley broth. When he left, we wandered out into the large yard. There were several rows of barracks just like ours. Some did not have wooden floors, and the refugees in those were forced to sleep on dirt covered by the dirty straw. There was nothing left in the yard. Even the trees and shrubs had been pulled up and thrown outside the fence. There was to be no comfort for the people being housed in this prisoner of war camp.

On the second night there, a teenage boy attempted to escape over the fence. He didn't get far before he was shot and killed. Everyone was stunned.

There was a latrine at the end of each barrack, with one commode and five showers. Thirty-six families had been put in this one room. There were no partitions. A schedule was set up for the women to use the facilities at one time and then the men. Several families had to use the latrines and showers at the same time. There was no soap and the water was not heated. There were no shower curtains. But, at least we could stay clean. My frostbite was hurting most of the time. The rough straw did not make a comfortable bed. Dad spread his coat for Lilly and me to sleep on, but it was hard to get any sleep. There were so many people crowded into that one room, that it was never quiet. Small children cried from hunger and fear, as did many grown-ups. I'd pretend I was resting in a warm bath that soothed my frostbite. The Danish soldiers had taken away the ointment the doctor had given my mom.

After several weeks, each family was given one rickety bunkbed. However, there was no mattress — only more dirty straw. Lilly and I shared the narrow upper bunk, while mom and dad the bottom. It wasn't much improvement, but at least it was something. Dad hoped that the other barracks that had dirt floors had also received bunkbeds.

The barley broth was little more than dirty water. Bits of twigs, leaves and other odd things were found in this meager food we were forced to eat. People became weak from hunger and many died — the ill, elderly and the small children mostly. The Danish soldiers took the bodies away and the families never knew what happened to them. I suppose the family said prayers, but there was no service or mourning — only an attitude of "thank God it was over" for that person. I'm sure we all expected to die shortly.

I think it was the Red Cross that was our salvation. They visited our camp and were able to bring about a few changes. The food improved a little, but thin barley broth was the main staple. Sometimes we'd be given a basket of apples that were carefully passed out among us. I remember the first one I was given. I ate it very slowly. I even ate the core and then I sucked on the seeds. Nothing has ever tasted better to me.

The Red Cross contacted agencies in the United States trying to get some relief for us. After a few months, each family received a small C.A.R.E. — Committee on American Relief in Europe — package. Ours had a few tins of food, some utensils, vaseline for my frostbite, heavy white socks for my feet and a couple of blankets. We thought we were wealthy. The food did not last long, but it raised our spirits. We found the strength to become human again and to be determined to survive.

The most important thing the Red Cross did for us was to attempt to locate relatives or friends in Germany. This became crucial later when we could be released if we had a sponsor that would take us in and provide our fare to wherever they lived. Most of the people in the camp had also been displaced during the war and had no idea where their relatives were. It took many years after the war ended for families to reunite or learn the fate of loved ones. This was true in all of Europe and among all nationalities. Many, many people were never located.

My dad urged us all to go outside each day — to breathe the fresh air and soak up the sunshine. The weather was still warm and we could see the hills and trees in the distance. I kept wondering if I'd ever get beyond that fence again. Several other people had been shot trying to escape. The fence wasn't too high and there were holes where people could crawl through. But the soldiers were waiting on the outside to shoot anyone who tried. One whole family was killed as they tried to escape. Everyone was desperate, and many families talked about their chances of getting through. I don't know if anyone actually made it. Dad made sure we all stayed well away from the fence.

The Danish soldiers had set up some rules that we

were supposed to "govern" ourselves by. They appointed someone in each barracks to be in charge of the distribution of the food, distribution of mail and packages (after we started getting some), schedules for use of the latrines and showers, "play periods" for children, and a school that all children were supposed to attend. There were teachers among the refugees and they welcomed the chance to be with the children. The Red Cross arranged a few books, pencils and paper, but the teaching consisted mainly of story telling and remembrances of our lives before we fled the Russians. Each student got to talk and tell about their home and friends. I told about Fresco and my animals, and about my grandma and grandpa and Ervin. I was afraid they'd laugh when I told them about my magic birch trees. They didn't. Everyone had a special place they remembered. Dad taught geography to the children. He used chalk to draw the countries he talked about on the cement walks outside and everyone tried to be careful not to walk on them.

I began to make some friends among the other children. The frostbite still hurt and I couldn't play with them for long. We made up games and actually found ways to have fun. One of the mothers made a ball from old rags and string that came in a C.A.R.E. package. That ball was used for a lot of different kinds of games. One boy from our barrack became a special friend of mine. His name was Werner and we spent many hours together.

Werner
My Story

My name is Werner Mertz. I first knew Hildegard at the second concentration camp my family was sent to in 1945. The war had ended by then and it was the Danish that imprisoned us this time. The first time we were imprisoned by the Germans, even though we had been given German citizenship the previous year. We were from Poland and because my father was a policeman, our family was allowed to become German citizens, which was supposed to protect us. Our German citizenship got my mother and us children out of Poland just ahead of the advancing Russians. We got out on the last train from Poland. The Russians were right behind us. We heard them shooting. We were lucky. Two of my aunts never made it to that last train and they were killed. We were shipped to Berlin to stay with a German family for two weeks, but then we were all put into a German concentration camp. The war was still on and as far as we knew, the Germans were winning. My mother kept trying to find out why we were put in a concentration camp when we were Germans, and I think she was told we were still Polish. I was eight years old. My older sister was ten, my younger brother four, and my baby sister was about nine months old.

Like Hildegard and her family, we also traveled in an open wagon to catch that last train to leave Poland. It was only about fifteen miles from our home and my dad rode his motorcycle along beside us until we reached the station. He wanted to be sure we got there safely. He told us good-bye and went back to the town where we had lived all my life. We found out later he was killed immediately — not by the Russians but by the Polish townspeople that had not been granted German citizenship. He was a policeman — not a soldier!

The German concentration camp was bad enough but it was nothing compared to the Danish one in Aalborg. It was cruel. We had no food other than watery barley broth for weeks at a time, no beds or blankets or anything other than the clothes we were wearing. The rough wooden floor was covered with dirty straw, full of bugs and mice. Each family was assigned a small section to stay in. I'll never forget the horror of that place and the conditions we were forced to live in. We were hungry all the time — so hungry that our stomachs ached and were swollen. Later, the Danes gave each barrack a large kettle so the women could cook the broth. It wasn't much help, because they had to add a lot of water to the little bit of barley to make enough broth to go around. If it were a special occasion, such as Christmas, we'd get a few potatoes and maybe some vegetables. But never enough to to make the broth good. After the Red Cross visited us, we got apples once in a while. What a treat. I still love apples, but those that we got in that concentration camp were the best I've ever tasted.

Hildegard's and my mother became close friends. Her cousin, Lilly, and my older sister, Louise, also became good friends. The four of them took turns holding Waltraut, my little sister. Before we got shipped to Aalborg, she had been the cutest little girl you ever saw. She was always happy and giggling. I used to play with her and take her for wagon rides around the garden. She had a red wooden wagon that had been mine when I was little. She loved it. Now she was dying and there was nothing anyone could do for her. She was starving to death. She was so weak she couldn't even cry. The Danish soldiers just shrugged their shoulders and

Berta Mertz holding nine month old Waltraut, surrounded by her three other children at home in Poland — 1944

walked away when my mother begged them to give her some milk. One day, she died. She was one year old. It was my birthday. I was nine years old.

Hildegard's family and ours were the only mourners when Waltraut died. So many people in the concentration camps were dying that additional sorrow didn't seem to be something our fellow prisoners could express. Just a quiet, "I'm so sorry," was all anyone said. It seemed to be what the adults said to each other when a loved one died — and most families lost at least one person. My sister and Lilly tried to console each other and Hildegard just took my hand and held it for a moment. I knew what she meant to say to me, but she just couldn't say it.

Our barrack had become less crowded. Hildegard and her family were already there when we arrived and were assigned to that barrack. The Danish soldier told us where our section was and that became our home for over two years. We were in pretty bad shape physically when we got there, but after the Red Cross became involved with our welfare, food and medicine improved a little. If someone became very ill, a soldier would take them to a hospital and a doctor would look at them. They gave Hildegard something to treat her frostbite, but it didn't help much. No one was ever kept in a hospital or anything like that. But, at least it was something. I have always wondered if a doctor had looked at Waltraut, would he have given her milk and food that would have kept her alive?

Waltraut is buried somewhere in Denmark, but we were never able to find out where.

Soon after Waltraut died, new prisoners were trans-ferred to our camp from somewhere else in Denmark. Hildegard's Uncle Otto, Aunt Kate and their daughter, Elly, were among the new arrivals.

My Uncle Otto, Aunt Kate and Elly

The weather had turned cold and we were staying in the barrack most of the time. I was trying to stay warm. We wore our coats and shoes all the time. I wore my white socks and slippers. No one wore shoes in the summer months in order to save them. That afternoon, dad had been near the door watching the newcomers being herded into the barracks. Most of them looked very thin and ill. We wondered where they had come from. Suddenly, we saw daddy gently leading some people over to us. The lady looked so frail and hardly able to walk. Mom jumped up and rushed to them and they all began hugging and crying. I recognized my Aunt Elly first. She looked so different, but her smile was the same and when she spoke my name, and said, *mein schatz,* I knew who she was. I felt joy for the first time since we left the farm. I couldn't believe my happiness as I clung to her and cried. She pried me from her and said, "Look, there is more for you to be happy about. Don't you recognize your Uncle Otto and Aunt Kate?" I was so stunned. Uncle Otto held me close and called me all of the wonderful names he had for me whenever he'd visit grandpa. Daddy had lowered Aunt Kate to the floor and gently laid her back on his coat. She was very ill and tired, but she took my hand and smiled at me. I did not recognize her. The last time I saw Aunt Kate, my mother had said she weighed over 190 pounds, but looked trim and fashionable because she was well "corsetted." This Aunt Kate weighed less than 90 pounds.

Uncle Otto owned a large and properous ranch in Austria. As the Russians advanced, they also had to flee. They had traveled by train to Hamburg. They left Austria before we fled when there was still public transportation. They were treated quite well in Hamburg, where they shared an apartment with two other families. They had plenty of good food until the war ended. Uncle Otto had been a wealthy man and he had taken money with them when they fled. Finally, they were sent into Denmark for safety from the advancing Russian army, which was marching toward Berlin. In Denmark, they stayed in a small hotel in Arhus, overlooking the water. They were more comfortable than we were in our hotel in Alpenrade. But, when the war ended, they received even worse treatment than we suffered. Everything they owned was taken from them by the Danish soldiers and they were thrown into a small concentration camp in that city.

Aunt Elly, who was in her early twenties, received deplorable abuse from the soldiers. There was no escape for them. The food consisted of boiled rats, nails and other unspeakable things. Aunt Kate could not eat the food and they had very little water. They all became ill and did not expect to survive. It was as if the Danish soldiers intended to kill them by starvation. It was only after a visit by the Red Cross that their food improved to the same watery barley broth we received. But so many — like Aunt Kate — had lost any will to live. So many people had died in that prisoner of war camp that the soldiers decided to close it and send the remaining prisoners to other camps.

Aunt Kate was taken to visit a doctor in the nearby town. Usually, no one else was allowed to accompany the ill person, but because Aunt Kate was so weak, Uncle Otto went with her. He was more bitter after the doctor examined Aunt Kate. The doctor had diagnosed her as *only* being malnourished and would probably die soon, and shrugged his shoulders at her condition. Uncle Otto said he was a monster and if he had had the strength, he'd have hit him. The doctor gave her a bottle of tonic, but it didn't seem to do her any good. She lay near death for several weeks. Aunt Elly and my mom took care of her and encouraged her to live. Someone in the family held her hand and talked to her all the time she was awake. I would take my turn holding her very thin hand and singing her the songs grandpa had taught us. She kept her eyes closed most of the time, but she smiled and I knew she was listening to me. She finally started to recover. Aunt Kate never became strong again while we were in the concentration camp, but finally she was able to walk. Uncle Otto said it was the love of the family that gave her the will to live. Dad kept telling all of us to hold on and have faith that this life would end someday.

Uncle Otto became a second grandpa to me. He filled a special spot in my life that was missing since we had to leave grandpa in Kebbeln. He seemed to know when I needed encouragement and comfort, even though I was trying hard not to complain about my frostbite, being hungry, or missing the farm so much. He told me a lot of stories about grandpa when he was young and the fun they had as boys. They were brothers. Uncle Otto and Aunt Kate are my great uncle and aunt, and Aunt Elly is my mother's cousin. Mom and Elly were good friends when they were growing up.

Uncle Otto had spent several years in Wisconsin in the United States before the war. He came back when the war started to try to get his family out of Germany, but he was too late and not allowed to leave again. He was too old to serve in the army, but his ranch "served the Fatherland".

Uncle Otto was an engineer, but he had some knowledge of medicine and was able to tell us why the frostbite had turned my skin dark. He said the black was actually clotted blood. Profound damage had been done to the nerve endings and blood vessels. This is why my skin felt numb and tingled all the time. It only hurt a lot when I touched it or something rubbed against it. My feet hurt most. My dad said he thought the frostbite on my feet was probably worse than on my fingers or face because I had been walking on the icy potato plants prior to my getting on the wagon. My feet were probably cold and damp and never warmed while we were fleeing. I had gotten better, but as the black skin sluffed off, the new skin formed and left a whitish scar. It became very sensitive and itched every time this happened. Uncle Otto said frostbite was very much like an electrical burn. He watched my toes and fingers carefully and was pleased that I was not going to lose any of them. He was especially concerned with infection. He said it was remarkable, seeing the extent of the frostbite damage. I still wore my slippers and large clean socks. Eventually, someone gave me a pair of canvas shoes that were too large, but at least I had shoes to wear.

Prisoner of War Children

Werner and I made friends with most of the other children in the camp. As children will everywhere, we found things to do. The children made up games with the ball Werner's mother had made and a stick found in the yard provided a means of hitting their ball quite a distance. Another favorite game was to dig a small hole and place a little piece of wood across it. Each player would snap it up and the one who could shoot it the farthest would win. Some of the bigger boys got very good at this game. Because we were always so hungry, no one had a lot of energy. There was no quarreling among us children. Each seemed to feel responsibility for the other, and no one wished to harm another physically or to hurt their feelings. Everyone had bad days of feeling despondent and their fellow playmates tried to cheer them up. In many ways, the children adapted to their life as prisoners better than the adults. Because of their hunger, most of the children were serverly malnourished. They got used to having their friends die. The old and the infants died first — then the children.

School was mandatory for all children, but there was not too much learning. Werner had gone to school in Poland and only read Polish, so he appreciated the chance to learn to read German. The few books the Red Cross had gotten for the camp were not adequate to teach the many grades the children would have been in. Most of us got to know our numbers very well — addition, subtraction and multiplication — because these were things we could recite each day. The older children helped the younger with their schooling.

Storytelling was the main activity. I told lots of stories about the farm I'd lived on and my animals. Werner said he'd sure love to have a horse like Fresco to ride. Werner told us his family had lived in a big house in town. He said they had a large garden where his mother raised vegetables and flowers. They'd have picnic lunches in the garden. They were a happy family. He'd already told about his dad, and how he rode his motorcycle to the train station with them. After the prisoners were able to send and receive mail, Mrs. Mertz was finally able to find out what happened to him. She wrote to a Polish undertaker in that town asking if he knew anything about her husband. The undertaker wrote back in Polish saying he had buried him soon after they'd left, but he didn't know how he was killed. He said there were six or seven people buried in the same grave; they just threw them in. That's how they buried everyone who wasn't German.

One of the younger girls told us they had lived in Czechoslovakia. The Nazis SS had shot her father. She was only two at the time. Her mother tried to cross the mountain into Germany during the winter. During the previous summer, her dad had carried her in a backpack as the three of them hiked into those mountains on vacation. At the border was a cabin for tourists and her mother told the guards she was to be a cook for the cabin. After a few days, her mother was caught and they were sent to a concentration camp in Germany. She didn't know why or how they were sent to Denmark and ended up in a Danish concentration camp. All the school students had a story to tell, but mainly about their lives before the war ended.

The children's choir was the joy of the entire camp. The adults also sang, but the children had their own choir. They sang the old traditional songs, and some new ones that some adults would teach to the director. They sang in harmony and it was really beautiful. Of course, there was no musical instrument to accompany the choir, but they did very well without any. The director, Herr Frederick, had been a music teacher in the town of Bayreuth, not too far from Czechoslovakia. His baby son had been one of the first to die in our barrack, and his wife died soon after. He was very patient with us children and made us practice each line over and over until we had it perfect. We didn't mind. The children's choir is a memory that has stayed with the prisoners throughout our lives.

Christmas became special because of the children's choir. We'd learned to harmonize on most of the traditional Christmas music and many of the parents broke into tears when they heard us. Of course, there were no real presents or decorations, but I remember those Christmases as being wonderful. My mom found a German flag and made me a special "Sunday" dress. She sewed it by hand. It had short sleeves with a full skirt and sash. It was real pretty. I wore it on Christmas. That was the Christmas when we found some chewy candy wrapped in yellow paper in our C.A.R.E. package. There were only a few pieces to pass around, but they tasted so good. Uncle Otto said the C.A.R.E. package had been sent from Michigan and he thought the candy was salt water taffy. None of us had ever tasted it before.

Church services were held in the school room every

Sunday and everyone attended. There was no real minister or priest, but several parents took turns relating what they remembered from the Bible. The children's choir sang at the church services and the adults usually joined in. It was a time when all the prisoners from the various barracks got together. Church services were not held during the coldest times of winter — just as school was not held. No one had enough warm clothing to go out of their barrack. Clothes were shared and handed down, but no one had much — just a few comforts that arrived in a C.A.R.E. package.

One day someone stole the soap out of the showers and Werner got blamed for it. This was serious and some of the adults wanted to punish him. His mother wouldn't let them touch him, but she spanked him — the first he had gotten since they left Poland. It was very rough. He said he didn't do it. He insisted he wouldn't steal anything. I believed him, but some of the others didn't. Living together as we all were, it was hard on Werner and his mother to have people mistrust him. No one ever owned up to taking the soap, but a few days later, it showed up again in the showers.

Watching the soldiers on the outside of the barbed wire fence was a constant pastime for some of the older boys. They didn't seem to comprehend the seriousness of being locked up and guarded every minute. After the first couple of years in the camp, no one had tried to escape, so no one had been shot. They would talk about escaping, but where would they go? Without help on the outside, there was no chance of getting out of Denmark — that is, if they weren't shot by a guard.

One old plane was left in the barracks yard. It was just a shell of a fighter plane without an engine or any equipment. The children would climb on it, but most of the mothers didn't think it was safe. My father had found a way to cut some of the aluminum from the plane. He had twisted a small piece from the frame and made it into a knife. He sharpened it on a rock. He cut pieces of the aluminum for people that they shaped into spoons and other utensils. Werner's mother made a soup ladle with holes in the bottom. She could dish up the broth and distribute the few potatoes, barley or any other vegetable evenly among the many bowls of the prisoners. Other people made things from the aluminum that were helpful to everyone.

My father also used his knife to carve little toys for the children. There weren't too many pieces of wood around, but anytime a kid would find one, he'd take it to my father and he'd make something out of it. He made me a tiny little doll that I carried with me all the time. He perfected the stick used in "stick-over-the-hole" game. The stick would sail further when it was balanced and smooth. Even though dad only had one arm, he was handy at making things and would try to help everyone. There weren't many men in the camp, so my father's kindness was comforting to all the children.

My Uncle Otto became an uncle to all the children. They would come to him for attention, the same way he encouraged and comforted me. He'd tell us about the United States and the children that he knew there, and the kind of games they played. He made it sound so wonderful we all vowed to live in the United States someday. He taught me to speak English.

Denmark – The War Years

The Danish soldiers remained as cruel and filled with hatred for us as when they first made us prisoners. We had been there two and half years and nothing had improved for us other than what the Red Cross and the C.A.R.E. packages provided. Clean straw for the floor and bunkbeds had only been provided a couple of times. Brooms had been made from the straw and the room was kept reasonably clean. We still had rats and bugs, but we were able to keep them under control. Our diet of thin barley broth continued except for very rare occasions. We received no nourishment that would have given us strength. We children grew very little during those years. Children do not grow unless they are nourished. People continued to die and were taken away to be buried. The families never knew where. Now a brief service was held each Sunday during our church service for those that had died that week. Families mourned in private.

We received our precious C.A.R.E. packages from the United States and the few people who had been able to locate relatives received mail from them. We had not heard a radio or read a newspaper since the war ended. We did not know what was going on beyond the barbed wire that imprisoned us. We did not know of the holocaust and the death camps and the millions of people that had died there. Nor did we know of the terrible destruction of German cities, or cities in England, France, Italy, Russia and the rest of Europe. We had watched the destruction of Konigsberg and dad and Uncle Otto said they knew Germany had suffered terrible losses, and assumed other countries had, too.

One of the men with the Red Cross finally was able to talk with dad and Uncle Otto. Usually, whenever the Red Cross men and women had come to our camp, the soldiers would not let them converse with the prisoners other than to hand out the C.A.R.E. packages and to get information concerning relatives in Germany. They kept saying, *kein fraternisierend, kein fraternisierend,* (no fraternizing, no fraternizing). Herr Flanagan, a Swedish Red Cross worker, was shocked that dad and Uncle Otto knew nothing of what had happened since the surrender of Germany. One day they were able to talk for almost an hour.

Dad asked about the furious hate the Danes still had for us prisoners. He knew the Germans had been harsh on the civilians of every country they had invaded. But it was the war. The children in the concentration camp had not been involved in the atrocities of their country. Why continue to treat them so terribly? Herr Flanagan told them of the terrible suffering endured by Denmark and the Danish people for six years under Nazi occupation. He said they were bitter and blamed all Germans.

Denmark had declared itself neutral when the tragedy of the global cataclysm that involved 56 nations began with the first strike of the *Wehrmacht* into Poland in 1939. Hitler's war strategies were carefully implemented. Invading Denmark was essential to the Nazi's successful invasion of Finland and Norway. Hitler had to control the Baltic Sea. Denmark bordered Germany on the south. The two countries had shared many geographical and cultural advantages for centuries. Denmark was a peaceful country. The *Wehrmacht* and the *Luftwaffe* — the Nazis war machines — had rolled across Denmark, striking quickly and ruthlessly. The Danish King Christian X yielded with dispatch. It was April 8, 1939. The Danish people were stunned. They had been invaded by a "friendly" neighboring country. The Nazis imposed harsh rules, and quickly stripped the land of food and industrial materials needed by the German "Fatherland." Ships, trains, planes and all factories were confiscated. The Danish people faced starvation and depredation. The alleged atrocities included the immediate killing of the country's leaders that expressed opposition to the Nazi regime. Any resistance was retaliated with multiple killings. If a German soldier were attacked or killed, a dozen Danish people would be randomly selected and killed in retaliation. They murdered women and children along with the men. This wanton murder of the Danish people went on in the countrysides as well as the towns. When German soldiers and airmen brought their families to Denmark, homes were confiscated and given to them. Usually the former homeowners were pressed into service as servants to the new owners. Most Danes lost all their property. Former store owners — probably including the lady with the doll shop where Hildegard admired the dolls in the window — found themselves working for the Nazis. They earned a small wage that barely sustained them. In Alpenrade, the Danish people had not been friendly, but Hildegard had not found them mean. Perhaps it was due to her being a small child whose face showed the signs of painful frostbite. The townspeople had sympathy for her.

The mother of the little girl from Czechoslovakia said the atrocities in her country had been the same. Her husband had been a teacher. A German soldier had been killed so the Nazis took all the men teachers to the school yard and shot them, as the students looked on in horror. They wouldn't even give her his body. They said they were traitors to the Third Reich and didn't deserve a funeral. They were buried together in a common hole. She said her sister-in-law was married to a Jewish lawyer. The whole family, including two teenage children and a baby, had been put on a train. They never heard of them again. They'd heard rumors of gas chambers where train loads of Jews were sent. She didn't know if it were true.

Other adults spoke up and said they, too, knew of whole families being loaded onto the trains and that they were all dead. All the Jewish people, even those that had served with distinction in the German army during WWI, were sent to the death camps — including doctors, lawyers, teachers and other prominent citizens. Some small towns were left without a doctor.

Herr Flanagan sent a special C.A.R.E. package of magazines and newspapers to dad, which he kept hidden under his blanket, because such material was forbidden by the Danish soldiers. Herr Flanagan also promised a radio, if he could get one. They were not easy to get.

Dad, Uncle Otto and other adults read and reread the old newspapers and magazines. Two and a half years after the war ended, Europe was in chaos and we were still prisoners of war in Denmark. Germany had been divided into four zones — English, French, American and Russian. Berlin had been divided between the American and Soviet zones. We didn't know what zone Kebbeln would be in. Dad and Uncle Otto knew our fate depended on what country governed our homes. The United Nations had set up relief agencies throughout Europe to assist people in locating their families or to learn their fates. It was a monumental job. The Red Cross was our only hope of locating relatives who had survived the war and lived in a zone other than Russian. Relatives had to sponsor inmates and guarantee them a home, or they could not be released from the concentration camp. The Danes were willing to send us back — but neither the English, American nor French authorities would accept us. They had their hands full with millions of displaced people already. However, the United Nations continued to work with the Red Cross in trying to locate relatives for all the refugees interned in foreign countries. But our big problem was that, so far, the Red Cross had not located any of our relatives. What had happened to them? We were a large family.

Dad was saddened to learn of the atrocities by his fellow Germans. He became deeply depressed and fell quiet and withdrawn. Since fleeing from the farm, he had been the one to encourage the family to be brave and to hang on — all this would end someday. Now he didn't seem to care. It seemed to be only the love and concern for me, his little daughter, that brought any life back into his eyes. I talked to my mom about the change in dad, and she told me I could help him by staying near him and talking to him, and telling him how much I loved him and needed him in my life. I, too, became discouraged and thought we'd never be able to leave Alborg — I'd never see the farm and my birch trees again.

Late Fall – 1947

A few families had been able to leave Aalborg because they found relatives. The Red Cross handled all the forms and paper work for each person. You'd think it would be easy. Just open the barbed wire gates and let people get on a train and go home. It was not that easy. It was very frustrating to go through the red tape and anxiety of knowing you could go home, but be delayed because someone at a desk somewhere had not put a stamp of approval on a form. After almost three years of existing as a prisoner, it was cruel to wait even another week for freedom. We were so happy for our friends that were leaving, but we shared their anxiety also. The Red Cross provided food and transportation to their destinations in Germany for those that were lucky enough to leave. We had to wonder when, and if, our turn to leave the prisoner of war camp would ever come.

Finally we were told that my Aunt Irmgard and Uncle Fritz had been looking for us for two years. After the war ended they moved to Fellbach, a town near the Swiss border, and settled in a small apartment. They were in the French zone. Before the war, their home had been in Austria, which became part of the Russian zone. Communications were difficult and information was hard to get. Uncle Fritz contacted the United Nations in the French headquarters and listed everyone in the family. Every few weeks, he journeyed to the

United Nations' offices in the French zone, to see if there were any new information. It was confirmed that grandpa, Ervin and those left to defend Kebbeln from the Russians had been killed. It was also assumed that grandma and those left behind in Konigsberg had also been killed. There was no trace of them. Uncle Fritz was afraid that we'd been among those left on the dock as the *Deutschland* sailed, because there were almost no survivors of that group. He finally traced us to Flensburg and on to the hotel in Alpenrod, but the trail stopped there. No one knew we had been thrown into the Danish concentration camp. The Danes made no attempt to list the people they had imprisoned. No records were kept of those who died. It was only by chance that the name Otto Grimm appeared on a list that landed on the desk of an interpreter at the United Nations, that Uncle Fritz got his first glimmer of hope. He went back for several days to search the entire list. He found the name of Otto Grimm's wife, Kate. Finally he found the names of Ernst Schmidt, his wife, Herta, daughter, Hildegard and a niece, Lilly Kausch.

He had found us.

Uncle Fritz suffered more frustration as he realized he had no way to communicate with us. We didn't have an address, so he couldn't write to us. It took several weeks for him to locate "our" Red Cross workers and to be able to send us a letter through them. The joy of receiving that letter will never leave my mind. We knew we would be saved.

The first letter from Uncle Fritz was brief. After he told us Aunt Irmgard and little Edertraut were safe and well, he outlined the procedures he would go through to get us released to him in Fellbach. It was complicated. He had to prove that we were related, but their passports, identification, and other papers that would have proved who they were had been confiscated in their flight across Germany after the war ended. Of course, we had nothing. I don't know how it was finally proved that we really were related, but I know the Red Cross worked on our behalf. I think they asked verbal questions of Uncle Otto and my dad and confirmed them by Uncle Fritz in Fellbach. The Red Cross was the go-between.

It worked. We were declared related and told we could leave for Fellbach.

We said good-bye to the people we had lived with so long. It was especially hard for me to say good-bye to Werner. None of his relatives had been found so far in Poland.

It was September 18, 1947. Thirty-two months had passed since we fled the farm in Kebbeln. We were given a box lunch and our train tickets by the Red Cross. My dad, mom, Lilly, Uncle Otto, Aunt Kate, Aunt Elly and I walked the short distance to the train station. It was the first time since May 8, 1945 that any of us had been beyond the barbed wire fence. The soldiers with their rifles watched us leave.

I was ten and a half years old. I was able to wear my canvas shoes that had once been too large for me.

Epilogue

The refugees from the prisoner of war camp in Aalborg Vestre Alle, Denmark, suffered additional indignities and hardships as they returned to Germany, their homeland. They were not welcomed. They were "displaced persons." This was the term used worldwide for destitute people returning home. People who had lost everything. The Schmidt family had no money, no home, no jobs, and no means of supporting themselves. It didn't matter that the family had owned a prosperous farm and were highly respectible people in their community prior to their fleeing in 1944. It didn't matter that they had survived almost three years of unthinkable hardship in a filthy prisoner of war camp — endured illness, hunger, and death. The German people who had survived the war and had spent the last three years of peacetime rebuilding their lives, didn't want to be burdened by their fellow countrymen who were less fortunate. And there was no aid available to assist those who needed it so desparately. Fritz and Irmard did not have room to house the six refugees. They assisted as well as they could, but it was apparent that Ernst Schmidt would have to find work and housing for his family quickly. The family was placed in yet another camp for war refugees where they had a roof over their heads. However, they were not prisoners. They were free to come and go as they pleased and they slowly began to rebuild their lives. Finally, the family found a one room apartment in the town of Vertenburg. It was owned by the Catholic nuns who befriended the family. Hildegard was enrolled in the Catholic school where she excelled in history and geography, thanks in part to the atlas game her dad played with her. She also was fairly fluent in English, thanks to the teaching of Uncle Otto. Ernst and Herta Schmidt found work on a farm which gave them a little money to buy food. Ernst worked with the animals and Herta cooked. Hildegard was primarily left on her own. She found a job on another farm after school where she dug potatoes and took care of the cows. Her pay was all the fruit she wanted to eat and a small amount to take home. Every little bit helped.

The nuns were very good to the little girl who still suffered from frostbite. It was healing, but her face continued to be blotched with dark skin. She still wore donated clothes with her white socks and tennis shoes. One day the nuns surprised Hildegard with a beautiful new dress with blue and white ruffles, and a matching pair of shoes. It is hard to imagine what this gift meant to a young girl who had so little. She was also given a little Catholic Bible with pictures. Although the family was Lutheran, she attended the Catholic School and Church. Hildegard joined the choir and discovered she had a very nice voice. She sang solo at the midnight mass. She did well in school. For the first time in many years, Hildegard was happy!

Another dream came true for Hildegard. Herta Schmidt became pregnant, and after a very dangerous delivery, where she remained in a coma for many days, a baby brother was brought home to Hildegard. She was filled with joy. Since her mother was too weak to care for the wee one, she immediately took charge and became the primary care giver of Baby John. She became his mother and took wonderful care of him. The nuns gave them baby clothes and a little baby buggy. The town soon got used to seeing Hildegard proudly pushing her baby brother wherever she went.

Ernst Schmidt finally got a good job as an accountant

in another town called Ehingen and the family had to move. Even though it meant a good salary, a larger apartment and more of the necessities of life, Hildegard was devastated. She hated to leave the tiny apartment, the nuns, her school and her teacher. It meant starting over again among people who looked on them as "displaced persons."

One of the advantages of this new home in Ehingen was the nearness of other family members. Her remaining grandma, who had fled earlier in 1944 with other family members, lived within five miles. Edeltraut was close enough to visit often and to stay over the weekends. The two girls renewed their love for each other and in spite of the age differences, spent as much time together as possible. There was no public transportation they could afford, so all the family members walked the five miles distance between them.

Hildegard continued to do well in school and graduated with honors from a business school. She got a job, moved into her own rooms, and was on her own for the first time in her life. She met and married an American soldier who was stationed in Ehingen and continued to live there until her husband was transfered back to the States. They ended up in Ypsilanti, Michigan where she has raised her two sons.

Grandpa Schmidt — One of the most remarkable stories to emerge from this episode is that of Grandpa Schmidt. The German soldiers had made him and eight year old Ervin remain in Kebbeln to face the Russians as the rest of his family fled in 1944. His son, Ernst Schmidt, was told after the family's release from the prisoner of war camp in 1947 that both Grandpa and Ervin had been killed along with the other civilians left to defend the "Fatherland."

Grandpa Schmidt was not killed. He survived.

The Russians did not kill Mr. Schmidt because he was useful to them. He was a prisoner in his workshop and was made to produce things for the Russian Army. After the war, he was not allowed to leave Russia — Kebbeln was in the Russian Zone. He existed, but little more. He did not know where any of his family was and had no way to search for them. He was held in Kebbeln for over twenty years. He became an old man.

In the late 1960s, the Red Cross obtained permission for him to leave. But they needed to locate a relative. Hildegard was in the United States and other family members were scattered. Eventually, Ernst Schmidt was located in Germany and Grandpa Schmidt was reunited with his son and remaining family. It was a joyous reunion, although the old man could not remember any of them. Nor could he remember what happened to his son's farm in Kebbeln.

Hildegard flew to Germany to see her Grandpa. He didn't recognize her as a grown woman. Finally, she pierced his memory by singing the songs to him that he had sung to her as a child. His face brightened and he whispered, *"Liebling, mein schatz,* (my little love, my treasure) — the words he'd whispered to her as she fled in the wagon twenty-two years earlier.

Lilly Kausch, who had lived on the farm in Kebbeln, shared the flight from the Russians, and the years in the prisoner of war camp with Hildegard's family, was placed in a farm home. These people were very kind to her and treated her as their own. They lived only six miles from the town where the Schmidts lived and they visited often. Hildegard and Lilly remained close, even after Hildegard married and moved to the United States. Lilly married, had children and lived with her husband in Hamburg. She died in 1995.

Otto and Kate Grimm also lived close by to the town the Schmidt family had moved to. Uncle Otto's prosperous ranch in Austria was never returned to him. He was able to start another business and they lived comfortably. Aunt Kate never regained her health. She never weighed more than 95 pounds. She died after a few years. Uncle Otto never returned to the United States and he followed his wife in death within a decade.

Werner Mertz and his family spent several more months as prisoners of war in the camp in Denmark after Hildegard and her family were released. Finally, the Red Cross helped to locate a relative in Rometsch, Germany and they were released to him. Berta Mertz had written to the mayor of the town and asked if there were any people living there by the name of Mertz. Werner's great grandfather had immigrated there from Poland in 1846 and built a factory in the town. They hoped a distant relative might be found. The mayor located a relative by the name of Mertz who wrote to Berta, and the family's release was arranged through the Red Cross. Werner, his mother, sisters and brother went to Rometsch, Germany, which was in the French Zone. They, too, found themselves "displaced persons" and not welcome in Rometsch. The newly found relatives helped them get settled in a small apartment next to another refugee family. They began to rebuild their lives. Werner's siblings suffered from malnutrition, as did most of the refugee children. However, Werner was relatively health, which helped him to adjust to his new life more easily than the rest of his family.

His mother started to look for other members of the family. Through the Red Cross and the facilities of the United

Nations, some of her remaining family were located in the American Zone. Werner's grandfather, who had had a mill in Poland before the war, escaped into Germany, as did additional family members. His father's two sisters were shot trying to escape. These relatives in the American Zone were also "displaced persons" and their living conditions were no better than their relatives in the French Zone.

Werner's grandfather had tried to locate the family, immediately after the war ended, but had lost all track of them when they were sent to the camp in Denmark. He was overjoyed to learn they were alive and in the French Zone. However, people could not cross the borders from one zone to another — even between the French and American zones. One night Berta took her children and sneaked into the American Zone to visit her father. They made it, but they had to sneak back into the French Zone. But the family had been reunited.

Werner had learned to read and write German in the camp and did well in the German school his mother enrolled her children in. He was placed in a lower grade because of the schooling he had missed, but was soon skipped ahead two years to be with children of his own age. He never returned to Poland.

As a teenager, Werner learned the trade of cabinet making. He found employment in Germany, but still remembered Uncle Otto's stories of the United States. He wanted to immigrate. His mother's sister had married an American GI in Germany, and when they were shipped back to the States, Werner started dreaming of joining them. They had told him of the opportunities in the United States for good cabinet makers, and they agreed to sponsor him. He was very eager for a new life in this land of opportunity. However, he had to wait two years until he finally received his papers permitting him to come to the States. By that time, his aunt and her husband lived in Kansas City. He had not learned to speak English before he immigrated, and soon found himself at a distinct disadvantage. His first job was washing bottles. He enrolled in a night class and learned English, which led to a better job in his trade as a cabinet maker.

To his dismay, he was drafted into the United States Army and returned to Germany to serve for two years. When he returned to the States, he moved to Michigan and pursued his chosen trade.

Hildegard and Werner — Herta Schmidt and Berta Mertz had formed a close friendship in Aalborg, the Danish prisoner of war camp. After both families were released, Berta searched for her friend Herta and finally found the family in Ehingen. The friendship continued throughout the years as their children grew up, married and made their own lives. Letters continued to flow between the mothers, but Hildegard and Werner had never communicated since they said goodbye in the camp. In the mid 1960s, the two mothers were surprised to learn that Hildegard and Werner were in the same state in the vast United States. They were both in Michigan. Hildegard and her boys were in Ypsilanti and Werner had settled with his wife and family in Frankenmuth — a distance of only 75 miles.

The friendship that started under such dire circumstances was renewed and has grown to a warm and lasting one. A fitting ending to Hildegard's story of being a child prisoner of WWII.